Oster Digital French Door Oven Cookbook for Beginners

1500-Day Easy and Delicious Recipes with Complete Guide Beginners to Bake, Air Fry, Broil, Toast, Pizza and Dehydrate.

Patience Ujana

Table of Contents

Introduction

The Oster Digital French Door Oven is one of the most versatile and advanced oven out there in the market. With this particular appliance, you will be able to effortlessly bake, toast, pizza or broil your meals to absolute perfection and with ease!

This Oster Digital French Door Oven Cookbook is comprised of a delicious collection of recipes that are suitable for all tastes. Each recipe is simple to make, full of flavor, and offers a healthier alternative to traditionally fried foods. Throughout the pages of this cookbook, you will discover a variety of savory, salty, and other delicious recipes.

Besides, this book is going to give you more than hundreds of awesome recipes so that you can learn how to cook enough meals to keep them easy and delicious. Also inside the book, you'll find all the information you'll need, and with this book, you can make your life easier, happier.

Chapter 1: Pork

Smoked Paprika Pork Loin Chops

Prep Time: 5 Minutes
Cook Time: 15 Minutes
Serves: 4

Ingredients:

- 1 pound (454 g) pork loin chops
- 1 tablespoon olive oil
- Sea saltand ground black pepper, to taste
- 1 tablespoon smoked paprika

Directions:

1.Start by preheating the air fryer to 400°F (205°C).

2.Place all ingredients in a lightly greased crisper tray.

3.Place the crisper tray in the corresponding position in the air fryer. Select Air Fry and cook the pork loin chops for 15 minutes, turning them over halfway through the cooking time.

4.Bon appétit!

Nutritional Value (Amount per Serving):

Calories: 276; Fat: 16.16g; Carb: 1.98g; Protein: 29.51g

Pork Roast with Paprika

Prep Time: 5 Minutes
Cook Time: 55 Minutes
Serves: 4

Ingredients:

- 1½ pounds (680 g) center-cut pork roast
- 1 tablespoon olive oil
- Sea salt and freshly ground black pepper, to taste
- 1 teaspoon garlic powder
- 1 teaspoon hot paprika
- ½ teaspoon dried parsley flakes
- ½ teaspoon dried rosemary

Directions:

1. Start by preheating the air fryer to 360°F (182°C).

2. Toss all ingredients in a lightly greased crisper tray.

3. Place the crisper tray in the corresponding position in the air fryer. Select Roast and cook the pork for 55 minutes, turning it over halfway through the cooking time.

4. Serve warm and enjoy!

Nutritional Value (Amount per Serving):

Calories: 385; Fat: 19.13g; Carb: 0.91g; Protein: 49.24g

Pork Spareribs

Prep Time: 5 Minutes
Cook Time: 35 Minutes
Serves: 4

Ingredients:

- 2 pounds (907 g) pork spareribs
- 1 teaspoon coarse sea salt
- ⅓ teaspoon freshly ground black pepper
- 1 tablespoon brown sugar
- 1 teaspoon cayenne pepper
- 1 teaspoon garlic powder
- 1 teaspoon mustard powder

Directions:

1. Start by preheating the air fryer to 350°F (180°C).

2. Toss all ingredients in a lightly greased crisper tray.

3. Place the crisper tray in the corresponding position in the air fryer. Select Roast and cook the pork ribs for 35 minutes, turning them over halfway through the cooking time.

4. Bon appétit!

Nutritional Value (Amount per Serving):

Calories: 552; Fat: 31.63g; Carb: 2.89g; Protein: 60.01g

Pork Belly with Tomato Sauce

Prep Time: 10 Minutes
Cook Time: 17 Minutes
Serves: 6

Ingredients:

- 1½ pounds (680 g) pork belly, cut into pieces
- ¼ cup tomato sauce
- 1 tablespoon tamari sauce
- 2 tablespoons dark brown sugar
- 1 teaspoon minced garlic
- Sea salt and ground black pepper, to taste

Directions:

1.Start by preheating the air fryer to 400°F (205°C).

2.Toss all ingredients in the crisper tray.

3.Place the crisper tray in the corresponding position in the air fryer. Select Air Fry and cook the pork belly for about 17 minutes, shaking crisper tray halfway through the cooking time.

4.Bon appétit!

Nutritional Value (Amount per Serving):

Calories: 609; Fat: 60.17g; Carb: 4.63g; Protein: 11.1g

Pork Cheese Burgers

Prep Time: 8 Minutes
Cook Time: 15 Minutes
Serves: 4

Ingredients:

- 1 pound (454 g) ground pork
- Sea salt and ground black pepper, to taste
- 1 tablespoon Italian herb mix
- 1 small onion, chopped
- 1 teaspoon minced garlic
- ¼ cup grated Parmesan cheese
- ¼ cup seasoned bread crumbs
- 1 egg
- 4 hamburger buns
- 4 teaspoons Dijon mustard
- 4 tablespoons mayonnaise

Directions:

1.Start by preheating the air fryer to 380°F (193°C).

2.In a mixing bowl, thoroughly combine the pork, spices, onion, garlic, Parmesan, bread crumbs, and egg. Form the mixture into four patties.

3.Arrange the patties in the crisper tray.

4.Place the crisper tray in the corresponding position in the air fryer. Select Air Fry and cook the burgers for about 15 minutes or until cooked through; make sure to turn them over halfway through the cooking time.

5.Serve the burgers with hamburger buns, mustard, and mayonnaise. Enjoy!

Nutritional Value (Amount per Serving):

Calories: 604; Fat: 34.64g; Carb: 30.97g; Protein: 39.82g

Cheese Pork with Mushrooms

Prep Time: 10 Minutes
Cook Time: 15 Minutes
Serves: 4

Ingredients:

- 1½ pounds (680 g) pork tenderloin
- Sea salt and ground black pepper, to taste
- 2 tablespoons olive oil
- 1 pound (454 g) mushrooms, sliced
- 2 ounces (57 g) blue cheese

Directions:

1.Start by preheating the air fryer to 400°F (205°C).

2.Toss the pork with salt, black pepper, and olive oil. Transfer the pork to a lightly greased crisper tray.

3.Place the crisper tray in the corresponding position in the air fryer. Select Air Fry and cook the pork for 10 minutes, turning them over halfway through the cooking time.

4.Top the pork with the mushrooms. Continue to cook for about 5 minutes longer. Top the warm pork with blue cheese.

5.Bon appétit!

Nutritional Value (Amount per Serving):

Calories: 693; Fat: 17.94g; Carb: 86.87g; Protein: 58.64g

Bacon Salad with Croutons

Prep Time: 15 Minutes
Cook Time: 16 Minutes
Serves: 5

Ingredients:

- 1 pound (454 g) bacon, cut into thick slices
- 1 head lettuce, torn into leaves
- 1 tablespoon chopped fresh chives
- 1 tablespoon chopped fresh tarragon
- 1 tablespoon chopped fresh parsley
- 2 tablespoons freshly squeezed lemon juice
- 2 garlic cloves, minced
- Coarse sea salt and ground black pepper, to taste
- 1 teaspoon crushed red pepper flakes
- 2 cups bread cubes

Directions:

1.Start by preheating the air fryer to 400°F (205°C).

2.Place the bacon in the crisper tray. Place the crisper tray in the corresponding position in the air fryer. Select Air Fry and cook the bacon for approximately 10 minutes, tossing crisper tray halfway through the cooking time; reserve.

3.Reduce the temperature to 390°F (199°C). Place the crisper tray in the corresponding position in the air fryer. Select Air Fry and cook the bread cubes for approximately 6 minutes or until the bread is toasted.

4.Toss the remaining ingredients in a salad bowl; top the salad with the bacon and croutons. Bon appétit!

Nutritional Value (Amount per Serving):

Calories: 331; Fat: 27.4g; Carb: 15.34g; Protein: 11.78g

Pork Sausage with Brussels Sprouts

Prep Time: 5 Minutes
Cook Time: 15 Minutes
Serves: 4

Ingredients:

- 1 pound (454 g) sausage links, uncooked
- 1 pound (454 g) Brussels sprouts, halved
- 1 teaspoon dried thyme
- 1 teaspoon dried rosemary
- 1 teaspoon dried parsley flakes
- 1 teaspoon garlic powder

Directions:

1.Start by preheating the air fryer to 380°F (193°C).

2.Place the sausage and Brussels sprouts in a lightly greased crisper tray.

3.Place the crisper tray in the corresponding position in the air fryer. Select Air Fry and cook the sausage and Brussels sprouts for approximately 15 minutes tossing crisper tray halfway through the cooking time.

4.Bon appétit!

Nutritional Value (Amount per Serving):

Calories: 343; Fat: 20.96g; Carb: 21.98g; Protein: 25g

Picnic Ham with Garlic

Prep Time: 5 Minutes
Cook Time: 1 Hour
Serves: 4

Ingredients:

- 1½ pounds (680 g) picnic ham
- 2 tablespoons olive oil
- 2 garlic cloves, minced
- 2 tablespoons rice vinegar
- 1 tablespoon tamari sauce

Directions:

1.Start by preheating the air fryer to 400°F (205°C).

2.Toss the ham with the remaining ingredients; wrap the ham in a piece of aluminum foil and lower it into the crisper tray.

3.Reduce the temperature to 375°F (190°C). Place the crisper tray in the corresponding position in the air fryer. Select Air Fry and cook the ham for about 30 minutes.

4.Remove the foil, increase the temperature to 400°F (205°C), and continue to cook for an additional 15 minutes or until cooked through.

5.Bon appétit!

Nutritional Value (Amount per Serving):

Calories: 238; Fat: 12.55g; Carb: 2.52g; Protein: 28.91g

Rosemary Pork Butt

Prep Time: 5 Minutes
Cook Time: 55 Minutes
Serves: 4

Ingredients:

- 1½ pounds (680 g) pork butt

- 1 teaspoon butter, melted

- 2 garliccloves, pressed

- 2 tablespoons chopped fresh rosemary

- Coarse sea salt and freshly ground black pepper, to taste

Directions:

1.Start by preheating the air fryer to 360°F (182°C).

2.Toss all ingredients in a lightly greased crisper tray.

3.Place the crisper tray in the corresponding position in the air fryer. Select Roast and cook the pork for 55 minutes, turning it over halfway through the cooking time.

4.Serve warm and enjoy!

Nutritional Value (Amount per Serving):

Calories: 466; Fat: 31.1g; Carb: 0.67g; Protein: 42.78g

Pork Loin Ribs with Zucchini

Prep Time: 10 Minutes
Cook Time: 37 Minutes
Serves: 4

Ingredients:

- 1½ pounds (680 g) pork loin ribs
- 2 cloves garlic, minced
- 1 tablespoon olive oil
- 4 tablespoons whiskey
- 1 teaspoon onion powder
- Sea salt and ground black pepper, to taste
- ½ pound (227 g) zucchini, sliced

Directions:

1. Start by preheating the air fryer to 350°F (180°C).

2. Toss the pork ribs with the garlic, olive oil, whiskey and spices; place the ingredients in a lightly greased crisper tray.

3. Place the crisper tray in the corresponding position in the air fryer. Select Roast and cook the pork ribs for 25 minutes, turning them over halfway through the cooking time.

4. Top the pork ribs with the sliced zucchini and continue cooking an additional 12 minutes. Serve immediately.

5. Bon appétit!

Nutritional Value (Amount per Serving):

Calories: 303; Fat: 13.25g; Carb: 7.28g; Protein: 37.25g

Pork Loin Roast

Prep Time: 10 Minutes
Cook Time: 15 Minutes
Serves: 4

Ingredients:

- 1½ pounds (680 g) top loin roasts, sliced into 4 pieces
- 2 tablespoons olive oil
- 1 teaspoon hot paprika
- Sea salt and ground black pepper, to taste
- 1 tablespoon Dijon mustard
- 1 teaspoon crushed garlic

Directions:

1.Start by preheating the air fryer to 400°F (205°C).

2.Place all ingredients in a lightly greased crisper tray.

3.Place the crisper tray in the corresponding position in the air fryer. Select Air Fry and cook the pork for 15 minutes, turning it over halfway through the cooking time.

4.Bon appétit!

Nutritional Value (Amount per Serving):

Calories: 457; Fat: 28.92g; Carb: 3.53g; Protein: 46.42g

Rib Roast with Tamari Sauce

Prep Time: 5 Minutes
Cook Time: 55 Minutes
Serves: 4

Ingredients:

- 1½ pounds (680 g) pork center cut rib roast

- 2 teaspoons butter, melted

- 1 teaspoon red chili powder

- 1 teaspoon paprika

- 1 teaspoon garlic powder

- ½ teaspoon onion powder

- Sea salt and ground black pepper, to taste

- 2 tablespoons tamari sauce

Directions:

1. Start by preheating the air fryer to 360°F (182°C).

2. Toss all ingredients in a lightly greased crisper tray.

3. Place the crisper tray in the corresponding position in the air fryer. Select Roast and cook the pork for 55 minutes, turning it over halfway through the cooking time.

4. Serve warm and enjoy!

Nutritional Value (Amount per Serving):

Calories: 382; Fat: 17.81g; Carb: 3.12g; Protein: 49.74g

Pork Ribs with Garlic

Prep Time: 5 Minutes
Cook Time: 35 Minutes
Serves: 4

Ingredients:

- 1½ pounds (680 g) St. Louis-style ribs

- 1 teaspoon hot sauce

- 1 tablespoon canola oil

- Kosher salt and ground black pepper, to taste

- 2 garlic cloves, minced

Directions:

1. Start by preheating the air fryer to 350°F (180°C).

2. Toss all ingredients in a lightly greased crisper tray.

3. Place the crisper tray in the corresponding position in the air fryer. Select Roast and cook the pork ribs for 35 minutes, turning them over halfway through the cooking time.

4. Bon appétit!

Nutritional Value (Amount per Serving):

Calories: 276; Fat: 13.13g; Carb: 1.65g; Protein: 35.65g

Scallions Pork Dinner Rolls

Prep Time: 10 Minutes
Cook Time: 15 Minutes
Serves: 4

Ingredients:

- 1 pound (454 g) ground pork
- Sea salt and freshly ground black pepper, to taste
- 1 teaspoon crushed red pepper flakes
- ½ cup chopped scallions
- 2 garlic cloves, minced
- 1 tablespoon olive oil
- 1 tablespoon soy sauce
- 8 dinner rolls, split

Directions:

1.Start by preheating the air fryer to 380°F (193°C).

2.In a mixing bowl, thoroughly combine the pork, spices, scallions, garlic, olive oil, and soy sauce. Form the mixture into four patties.

3.Arrange the patties in the crisper tray.

4.Place the crisper tray in the corresponding position in the air fryer. Select Air Fry and cook the patties for about 15 minutes or until cooked through; make sure to turn them over halfway through the cooking time.

5.Serve the patties in dinner rolls and enjoy!

Nutritional Value (Amount per Serving):

Calories: 538; Fat: 31.21g; Carb: 28.21g; Protein: 34.56g

Pork Tacos with Chiles

Prep Time: 10 Minutes
Cook Time: 55 Minutes
Serves: 4

Ingredients:

- 2 ancho chiles, seeded and minced
- 2 garlic cloves, chopped
- 1 tablespoon olive oil
- Kosher salt and freshly ground black pepper, to taste
- 1 teaspoon dried Mexican oregano
- 1½ pounds (680 g) pork butt
- 4 corn tortillas, warmed

Directions:

1. Start by preheating the air fryer to 360°F (182°C).

2. Toss all ingredients, except for the tortillas, in a lightly greased crisper tray.

3. Place the crisper tray in the corresponding position in the air fryer. Select Air Fry and cook the pork butt for 55 minutes, turning it over halfway through the cooking time.

4. Using two forks, shred the pork and serve in tortillas with toppings of choice. Serve immediately!

Nutritional Value (Amount per Serving):

Calories: 676; Fat: 36.06g; Carb: 39.08g; Protein: 47.77g

Bacon and Tomato Sandwich

Prep Time: 8 Minutes
Cook Time: 10 Minutes
Serves: 3

Ingredients:

- 6 ounces (170 g) thick-cut bacon
- 2 tablespoons brown sugar
- 2 teaspoons chipotle chile powder
- 1 teaspoon cayenne pepper
- 1 tablespoon Dijon mustard
- 1 heads lettuce, torn into leaves
- 2 medium tomatoes, sliced
- 6 (½-inch) slices white bread

Directions:

1.Start by preheating the air fryer to 400°F (205°C).

2.Toss the bacon with the sugar, chipotle chile powder, cayenne pepper, and mustard.

3.Place the bacon in the crisper tray. Place the crisper tray in the corresponding position in the air fryer. Select Air Fry and cook the bacon for approximately 10 minutes, tossing crisper tray halfway through the cooking time.

4.Assemble the sandwiches with the bacon, lettuce, and tomato.

5.Bon appétit!

Nutritional Value (Amount per Serving):

Calories: 345; Fat: 18.39g; Carb: 36.09g; Protein: 13.17g

Sausage Sandwich with Mustard

Prep Time: 5 Minutes
Cook Time: 15 Minutes
Serves: 3

Ingredients:

- 1 pound (454 g) sweet Italian sausage

- 6 white bread slices

- 2 teaspoons mustard

Directions:

1.Start by preheating the air fryer to 370°F (188°C).

2.Place the sausage in a lightly greased crisper tray.

3.Place the crisper tray in the corresponding position in the air fryer. Select Air Fry and cook the sausage for approximately 15 minutes, tossing crisper tray halfway through the cooking time.

4.Assemble the sandwiches with the bread, mustard, and sausage, and serve immediately.

5.Bon appétit!

Nutritional Value (Amount per Serving):

Calories: 361; Fat: 14.05g; Carb: 27.96g; Protein: 30.48g

Pork Loin Chops with Onions

Prep Time: 5 Minutes
Cook Time: 15 Minutes
Serves: 4

Ingredients:

- 1½ pounds (680 g) pork loin chops, boneless
- 2 tablespoons olive oil
- ½ teaspoon cayenne pepper
- 1 teaspoon garlic powder
- Sea salt and ground black pepper, to taste
- 1 onion, cut into wedges

Directions:

1.Start by preheating the air fryer to 400°F (205°C).

2.Place all ingredients in a lightly greased crisper tray.

3.Place the crisper tray in the corresponding position in the air fryer. Select Air Fry and cook the pork loin chops for 15 minutes, turning them over halfway through the cooking time.

4.Bon appétit!

Nutritional Value (Amount per Serving):

Calories: 449; Fat: 25.7g; Carb: 8g; Protein: 44.6g

Glazed Ham

Prep Time: 5 Minutes
Cook Time: 1 Hour
Serves: 4

Ingredients:

- 1½ pounds (680 g) smoked and cooked ham
- ¼ cup honey
- 1 small-sized orange, freshly squeezed
- 1 tablespoon balsamic vinegar
- 1 tablespoon stone-ground mustard
- ½ teaspoon crushed red pepper flakes
- Freshly ground black pepper, to taste

Directions:

1. Start by preheating the air fryer to 400°F (205°C).

2. In a mixing bowl, whisk all the remaining ingredients to make the glaze.

3. Wrap the ham in a piece of aluminum foil and lower it into the crisper tray. Reduce the temperature to 375°F (190°C). Place the crisper tray in the corresponding position in the air fryer. Select Air Fry and cook the ham for about 30 minutes.

4. Remove the foil, increase the temperature to 400°F (205°C), and continue to cook an additional 15 minutes, coating the ham with the glaze every 5 minutes.

5. Bon appétit!

Nutritional Value (Amount per Serving):

Calories: 263; Fat: 6.39g; Carb: 23.59g; Protein: 29.58g

Pork Cheese Sandwich

Prep Time: 10 Minutes
Cook Time: 55 Minutes
Serves: 4

Ingredients:

- 1½ pounds (680 g) pork butt

- 1 teaspoon stone-ground mustard

- ½ teaspoon ground cumin

- 2 cloves garlic, crushed

- Kosher salt and freshly ground black pepper, to taste

- ½ teaspoon ground allspice

- 2 tablespoons fresh pineapple juice

- 2 ounces (57 g) Swiss cheese, sliced

- 16 ounces (454 g) Cuban bread loaf, sliced

Directions:

1.Start by preheating the air fryer to 360°F (182°C).

2.Toss all ingredients , except for the cheese and bread, in a lightly greased crisper tray.

3.Place the crisper tray in the corresponding position in the air fryer. Select Air Fry and cook the pork butt for 55 minutes, turning it over halfway through the cooking time.

4.Using two forks, shred the pork; assemble the sandwiches with cheese and bread. Serve warm and enjoy!

Nutritional Value (Amount per Serving):

Calories: 821; Fat: 37.99g; Carb: 57.91g; Protein: 58.94g

Basil Pork Butt

Prep Time: 5 Minutes
Cook Time: 55 Minutes
Serves: 4

Ingredients:

- 1½ pounds (680 g) pork butt
- 1 teaspoon olive oil
- 1 teaspoon dried rosemary
- 1 teaspoon dried thyme
- 1 teaspoon dried oregano
- 1 teaspoon dried basil
- 1 teaspoon cayenne pepper
- Sea salt and ground black pepper, to taste

Directions:

1.Start by preheating the air fryer to 360°F (182°C).

2.Toss all ingredients in a lightly greased crisper tray.

3.Place the crisper tray in the corresponding position in the air fryer. Select Air Fry and cook the pork for 55 minutes, turning it over halfway through the cooking time.

4.Serve warm and enjoy!

Nutritional Value (Amount per Serving):

Calories: 472; Fat: 31.35g; Carb: 1.66g; Protein: 43g

Air Fried Sausage with Ginger

Prep Time: 5 Minutes
Cook Time: 15 Minutes
Serves: 4

Ingredients:

- 1 pound (454 g) Frankfurter sausage

- ¼ cup ginger ale

- 2 tablespoons liquid honey

- Red pepper flakes, to taste

Directions:

1. Start by preheating the air fryer to 370°F (188°C).

2. Place all ingredients in a lightly greased crisper tray.

3. Place the crisper tray in the corresponding position in the air fryer. Select Air Fry and cook the sausage for approximately 15 minutes, tossing crisper tray halfway through the cooking time.

4. Bon appétit!

Nutritional Value (Amount per Serving):

Calories: 306; Fat: 15.62g; Carb: 19.71g; Protein: 22.48g

Pork Patties with Teriyaki Sauce

Prep Time: 10 Minutes
Cook Time: 15 Minutes
Serves: 4

Ingredients:

- 1 pound (454 g) ground pork
- Kosher salt and ground black pepper, to taste
- 1 tablespoon chopped fresh parsley
- 1 tablespoon chopped fresh coriander
- 1 teaspoon sliced habanero pepper
- 1 tablespoon teriyaki sauce
- 1 small onion, chopped
- 1 clove garlic, minced
- 4 brioche hamburger buns, lightly toasted

Directions:

1.Start by preheating the air fryer to 380°F (193°C).

2.In a mixing bowl, thoroughly combine the pork, spices, habanero pepper, teriyaki sauce, onion, and garlic. Then, roll the mixture into four patties.

3.Arrange the patties in the crisper tray.

4.Place the crisper tray in the corresponding position in the air fryer. Select Air Fry and cook the pork patties for about 15 minutes or until cooked through; make sure to turn them over halfway through the cooking time.

5.Serve the patties with the brioche hamburger buns. Enjoy!

Nutritional Value (Amount per Serving):

Calories: 704; Fat: 39.27g; Carb: 39.96g; Protein: 47.24g

Pork Ribs with Tomato Sauce

Prep Time: 5 Minutes
Cook Time: 35 Minutes
Serves: 4

Ingredients:

- 1 tablespoon sesame oil
- 1½ pounds (680 g) back ribs
- ½ cup tomato sauce
- 1 tablespoon soy sauce
- 2 tablespoons agave syrup
- 2 tablespoons rice wine

Directions:

1.Start by preheating the air fryer to 350°F (180°C).

2.Toss all ingredients in a lightly greased crisper tray.

3.Place the crisper tray in the corresponding position in the air fryer. Select Air Fry and cook the pork ribs for 35 minutes, turning them over halfway through the cooking time.

4.Bon appétit!

Nutritional Value (Amount per Serving):

Calories: 485; Fat: 31g; Carb: 16.61g; Protein: 34.7g

Pork Rolls with Fish Sauce

Prep Time: 5 Minutes
Cook Time: 55 Minutes
Serves: 4

Ingredients:

- 1 pound (454 g) pork shoulder
- 1 tablespoon olive oil
- 2 cloves garlic, minced
- 1 teaspoon cayenne pepper
- 1 tablespoon chopped fresh sage
- 1 tablespoon chopped fresh thyme
- 1 tablespoon brown sugar
- 2 tablespoons fish sauce
- Kosher salt and freshly ground pepper, to taste
- 8 dinner rolls

Directions:

1.Start by preheating the air fryer to 360°F (182°C).

2.Toss all ingredients, except for thedinner rolls, in a lightly greased crisper tray.

3.Place the crisper tray in the corresponding position in the air fryer. Select Air Fry and cook the pork for 55 minutes, turning it over halfway through the cooking time.

4.Serve on dinner rolls and enjoy!

Nutritional Value (Amount per Serving):

Calories: 502; Fat: 27.12g; Carb: 29.28g; Protein: 33.94g

Bacon Squash and Eggplant Kebabs

Prep Time: 15 Minutes
Cook Time: 10 Minutes
Serves: 3

Ingredients:

- 1 tablespoon freshly squeezed lemon juice

- 1 teaspoon peeled and finely grated fresh ginger

- 1 tablespoon maple syrup

- ½ pound (227 g) bacon

- ½ pound (227 g) squash, diced

- ½ pound (227 g) eggplant, diced

- 1 large onion, cut into wedges

Directions:

1.Start by preheating the air fryer to 400°F (205°C).

2.Toss all ingredients in a mixing bowl until well coated on all sides.

3.Thread the ingredients onto skewers and place them in the crisper tray.

4.Place the crisper tray in the corresponding position in the air fryer. Select Air Fry and cook the skewers for approximately 10 minutes, turning them over halfway through the cooking time.

5.Serve warm with sauce on the side, if desired. Bon appétit!

Nutritional Value (Amount per Serving):

Calories: 322; Fat: 22.6g; Carb: 26.71g; Protein: 10g

Pork Gyros

Prep Time: 5 Minutes
Cook Time: 55 Minutes
Serves: 4

Ingredients:

- 1 pound (454 g) pork shoulder
- 1 teaspoon smoked paprika
- ½ teaspoon onion powder
- 1 teaspoon garlic powder
- ½ teaspoon ground cumin
- ½ teaspoon ground bay leaf
- Sea salt and ground black pepper, to taste
- 4 pitta bread, warmed

Directions:

1.Start by preheating the air fryer to 360°F (182°C).

2.Toss the pork on all sides, top and bottom, with the spices. Place the pork in a lightly greased crisper tray.

3.Place the crisper tray in the corresponding position in the air fryer. Select Air Fry and cook the pork for 55 minutes, turning it over halfway through the cooking time.

4.Shred the pork with two forks and serve on warmed pitta bread and some extra toppings of choice. Enjoy!

Nutritional Value (Amount per Serving):

Calories: 580; Fat: 23.56g; Carb: 51.77g; Protein: 37.8g

Fennel and Pork Souvlaki

Prep Time: 15 Minutes
Cook Time: 15 Minutes
Serves: 4

Ingredients:

- 1 tablespoon olive oil

- ½ teaspoon sweet paprika

- 1 pound (454 g) pork tenderloin, cubed

- 1 small lemon, freshly juiced

- 1 eggplant, diced

- 2 bell peppers, diced

- ½ pound (227 g) fennel,diced

Directions:

1.Start by preheating the air fryer to 400°F (205°C).

2.Toss all ingredients in a mixing bowl until well coated on all sides.

3.Thread the ingredients onto skewers and place them in the crisper tray.

4.Place the crisper tray in the corresponding position in the air fryer. Select Air Fry and cook the skewers for approximately 15 minutes, turning them over halfway through the cooking time.

5.Bon appétit!

Nutritional Value (Amount per Serving):

Calories: 256; Fat: 7.83g; Carb: 15.31g; Protein: 32.26g

Pork with Shaoxing Wine

Prep Time: 10 Minutes
Cook Time: 15 Minutes
Serves: 4

Ingredients:

- 1½ pounds (680 g) pork loin porterhouse, cut into 4 slices
- 1½ tablespoons sesame oil
- ½ teaspoon five-spice powder
- 2 garlic cloves, crushed
- 1 tablespoon soy sauce
- 1 tablespoon hoisin sauce
- 2 tablespoons Shaoxing wine

Directions:

1. Start by preheating the air fryer to 400°F (205°C).

2. Place all ingredients in a lightly greased crisper tray.

3. Place the crisper tray in the corresponding position in the air fryer. Select Air Fry and cook the pork loin chops for 15 minutes, turning them over halfway through the cooking time.

4. Bon appétit!

Nutritional Value (Amount per Serving):

Calories: 282; Fat: 14.56g; Carb: 6.49g; Protein: 32.25g

Spareribs with Sriracha Sauce

Prep Time: 5 Minutes
Cook Time: 35 Minutes
Serves: 5

Ingredients:

- 2 pounds (907 g) spareribs
- ¼ cup Sriracha sauce
- 1 teaspoon paprika
- Sea salt and ground black pepper, to taste

Directions:

1. Start by preheating the air fryer to 350°F (180°C).

2. Toss all ingredients in a lightly greased crisper tray.

3. Place the crisper tray in the corresponding position in the air fryer. Select Air Fry and cook the pork ribs for 35 minutes, turning them over halfway through the cooking time.

4. Bon appétit!

Nutritional Value (Amount per Serving):

Calories: 382; Fat: 16.68g; Carb: 1.97g; Protein: 52.68g

Sirloin Chops with Cheese

Prep Time: 5 Minutes
Cook Time: 15 Minutes
Serves: 3

Ingredients:

- 1 pound (454 g) sirloin chops
- 1 egg
- 2 tablespoons butter, at room temperature
- Sea salt and ground black pepper, to taste
- 3 tablespoons grated Pecorino cheese
- ½ cup bread crumbs
- 1 teaspoon paprika
- 1 teaspoon garlic powder

Directions:

1.Start by preheating the air fryer to 400°F (205°C).

2.Pat the pork sirloin chops dry with kitchen towels.

3.In a shallow bowl, whisk the egg until pale and frothy.

4.In another shallow bowl, thoroughly combine the remaining ingredients. Dip the pork chops into the egg, then the cheese and crumb mixture.

5.Place the pork sirloin chops in a lightly oiled crisper tray.

6.Place the crisper tray in the corresponding position in the air fryer. Select Air Fry and cook the pork sirloin chops for 15 minutes, turning them over halfway through the cooking time.

7.Bon appétit!

Nutritional Value (Amount per Serving):

Calories: 349; Fat: 18.38g; Carb: 7.14g; Protein: 37.21g

Rosemary Pork Belly

Prep Time: 5 Minutes
Cook Time: 45 Minutes
Serves: 5

Ingredients:

- 1 pound (454 g) pork belly
- 1 tablespoon tomato sauce
- 2 tablespoons rice vinegar
- 1 teaspoon dried thyme
- 1 teaspoon dried rosemary

Directions:

1.Start by preheating the air fryer to 320°F (160°C).

2.Toss all ingredients in a lightly greased baking pan.

3.Place the baking pan in the corresponding position in the air fryer. Select Bake and cook the pork belly for 20 minutes. Now, turn it over and continue cooking for a further 25 minutes.

4.Serve warm and enjoy!

Nutritional Value (Amount per Serving):

Calories: 115; Fat: 4.9g; Carb: 2.09g; Protein: 15.58g

Pork and Beef Burgers

Prep Time: 8 Minutes
Cook Time: 15 Minutes
Serves: 5

Ingredients:

- 1 pound (454 g) ground pork
- ½ pound (227 g) ground beef
- ½ cup chopped scallions
- 1 teaspoonminced garlic
- 1 tablespoon Sriracha sauce
- 5 tablespoons crushed tortilla chips
- 2 tablespoons olive oil
- Sea salt and ground black pepper, to taste
- 5 ciabatta rolls

Directions:

1.Start by preheating the air fryer to 380°F (193°C).

2.In a mixing bowl, thoroughly combine the meat, scallions, garlic, Sriracha sauce, tortilla chips, olive oil, salt, and black pepper. Form the mixture into four patties.

3.Arrange the patties in the crisper tray.

4.Place the crisper tray in the corresponding position in the air fryer. Select Air Fry and cook the burgers for about 15 minutes or until cooked through; make sure to turn them over halfway through the cooking time.

5.Serve the burgers with ciabatta rolls. Bon appétit!

Nutritional Value (Amount per Serving):

Calories: 696; Fat: 35.96g; Carb: 47.13g; Protein: 43.09g

Ham Steaks with Butter

Prep Time: 5 Minutes
Cook Time: 12 Minutes
Serves: 4

Ingredients:

- 1 pound (454 g) ham steaks

- 2 tablespoons butter, room temperature

- 1 teaspoon paprika

- 2 tablespoons agave syrup

Directions:

1.Start by preheating the air fryer to 380°F (193°C).

2.Place the ham in a lightly greased crisper tray.

3.Mix the butter, paprika, and agave syrup in a small bowl.

4.Place the crisper tray in the corresponding position in the air fryer. Select Air Fry and cook the ham steaks for about 4 minutes, turn them over and baste them with the butter glaze.

5.Cook for another 4 minutes, baste the ham steaks, and finally, cook an additional 4 minutes or until cooked through.

6.Bon appétit!

Nutritional Value (Amount per Serving):

Calories: 199; Fat: 9.71g; Carb: 9.86g; Protein: 19.31g

Bacon and Potato

Prep Time: 10 Minutes
Cook Time: 12 Minutes
Serves: 4

Ingredients:

- 1 pound (454 g) red-skinned potatoes, cut into 1-inch chunks
- Kosher salt and ground black pepper, to taste
- 1 pound (454 g) bacon, cut into thick slices
- 1 tablespoon chopped fresh chives
- 2 cloves garlic, minced

Directions:

1.Start by preheating the air fryer to 400°F (205°C).

2.Toss all ingredients in the crisper tray.

3.Place the crisper tray in the corresponding position in the air fryer. Select Air Fry and cook the bacon and potatoes for approximately 12 minutes, turning them over halfway through the cooking time.

4.Serve immediately. Bon appétit!

Nutritional Value (Amount per Serving):

Calories: 438; Fat: 33.67g; Carb: 26.79g; Protein: 14.6g

Sausage with Onion Rings

Prep Time: 5 Minutes
Cook Time: 15 Minutes
Serves: 4

Ingredients:

- 1 pound (454 g) pork sausage, smoked
- 4 ounces (113 g) onion rings

Directions:

1.Start by preheating the air fryer to 370°F (188°C).

2.Place the sausage in a lightly greased crisper tray.

3.Place the crisper tray in the corresponding position in the air fryer. Select Air Fry and cook the sausage for approximately 7 minutes, tossing crisper tray halfway through the cooking time.

4.Add in the onion rings and continue to cook for 8 minutes more. Bon appétit!

Nutritional Value (Amount per Serving):

Calories: 149; Fat: 6.13g; Carb: 4.26g; Protein: 19.66g

Pork with BBQ Sauce

Prep Time: 5 Minutes
Cook Time: 55 Minutes
Serves: 5

Ingredients:

- 2 pounds (907 g) pork butt

- 1 tablespoon olive oil

- Kosher salt and ground black pepper, to taste

- 1 teaspoon ground cumin

- ½ cup BBQ sauce

Directions:

1. Start by preheating the air fryer to 360°F (182°C).

2. Toss all ingredients in a lightly greased crisper tray.

3. Place the crisper tray in the corresponding position in the air fryer. Select Air Fry and cook the pork butt for 55 minutes, turning it over halfway through the cooking time.

4. Serve warm and enjoy!

Nutritional Value (Amount per Serving):

Calories: 521; Fat: 34.95g; Carb: 2.78g; Protein: 46.14g

Rosemary Pork Shoulder Chops

Prep Time: 5 Minutes
Cook Time: 15 Minutes
Serves: 4

Ingredients:

- 1½ pounds (680 g) pork shoulder chops

- 2 tablespoons olive oil

- Kosher salt and ground black pepper, to taste

- 2 sprigs rosemary, leaves picked and chopped

- 1 teaspoon crushed garlic

Directions:

1.Start by preheating the air fryer to 400°F (205°C).

2.Toss all ingredients in a lightly greased crisper tray.

3.Place the crisper tray in the corresponding position in the air fryer. Select Air Fry and cook the pork shoulder chops for 15 minutes, turning them over halfway through the cooking time.

4.Bon appétit!

Nutritional Value (Amount per Serving):

Calories: 285; Fat: 12.71g; Carb: 1.81g; Protein: 38.69g

Pork Ribs with Thyme

Prep Time: 5 Minutes
Cook Time: 35 Minutes
Serves: 4

Ingredients:

- 1½ pounds (680 g) baby back ribs
- 2 tablespoons olive oil
- 1 teaspoon smoked paprika
- 1 teaspoon garlic powder
- 1 teaspoon onion powder
- ½ teaspoon ground cumin
- 1 teaspoon mustard powder
- 1 teaspoon dried thyme
- Coarse sea salt and freshly cracked black pepper, to taste

Directions:

1.Start by preheating the air fryer to 350°F (180°C).

2.Toss all ingredients in a lightly greased crisper tray.

3.Place the crisper tray in the corresponding position in the air fryer. Select Air Fry and cook the pork ribs for 35 minutes, turning them over halfway through the cooking time.

4.Bon appétit!

Nutritional Value (Amount per Serving):

Calories: 448; Fat: 33.72g; Carb: 3g; Protein: 34.13g

Eggplant and Pork Skewers

Prep Time: 15 Minutes
Cook Time: 15 Minutes
Serves: 4

Ingredients:

- 1 pound (454 g) pork tenderloin, cubed
- 1 pound (454 g) bell peppers, diced
- 1 pound (454 g) eggplant, diced
- 1 tablespoon olive oil
- 1 tablespoon chopped parsley
- 1 tablespoon chopped cilantro
- Sea salt and ground black pepper, to taste

Directions:

1.Start by preheating the air fryer to 400°F (205°C).

2.Toss all ingredients in a mixing bowl until well coated on all sides.

3.Thread the ingredients onto skewers and place them in the crisper tray.

4.Place the crisper tray in the corresponding position in the air fryer. Select Air Fry and cook the skewers for approximately 15 minutes, turning them over halfway through the cooking time.

5.Bon appétit!

Nutritional Value (Amount per Serving):

Calories: 271; Fat: 7.82g; Carb: 18.53g; Protein: 33.31g

Pork with Herb

Prep Time: 5 Minutes
Cook Time: 55 Minutes
Serves: 5

Ingredients:

- 2 pounds (907 g) pork center cut
- 2 tablespoons olive oil
- 1 tablespoon Italian herb mix
- 1 teaspoon crushed red pepper flakes
- Sea salt and freshly ground black pepper, to taste

Directions:

1. Start by preheating the air fryer to 360°F (182°C).

2. Toss all ingredients in a lightly greased crisper tray.

3. Place the crisper tray in the corresponding position in the air fryer. Select Air Fry and cook the pork for 55 minutes, turning it over halfway through the cooking time.

4. Serve warm and enjoy!

Nutritional Value (Amount per Serving):

Calories: 285; Fat: 12.17g; Carb: 1.51g; Protein: 40.12g

Pork Sausage with Fennel

Prep Time: 5 Minutes
Cook Time: 15 Minutes
Serves: 4

Ingredients:

- 1 pound (454 g) pork sausage

- 1 pound (454 g) fennel, quartered

- 1 teaspoon garlic powder

- ½ teaspoon onion powder

- 2 teaspoons mustard

Directions:

1.Start by preheating the air fryer to 370°F (188°C).

2.Place all ingredients in a lightly greased crisper tray.

3.Place the crisper tray in the corresponding position in the air fryer. Select Air Fry and cook the sausage and fennel for approximately 15 minutes, tossing crisper tray halfway through the cooking time.

4.Bon appétit!

Nutritional Value (Amount per Serving):

Calories: 177; Fat: 6.42g; Carb: 10.84g; Protein: 21.01g

Pork Burgers

Prep Time: 15 Minutes
Cook Time: 15 Minutes
Serves: 4

Ingredients:

- 1 pound (454 g) ground pork
- 1 small onion, chopped
- 1 garlic clove, minced
- 4 tablespoons crushed tortilla chips
- 1 teaspoon minced fresh sage
- 1 teaspoon minced fresh coriander
- 1 tablespoon minced fresh parsley
- 1 egg, beaten
- ½ teaspoon smoked paprika
- Sea salt and freshly ground black pepper, to taste

Directions:

1.Start by preheating the air fryer to 380°F (193°C).

2.In a mixing bowl, thoroughly combine all ingredients . Form the mixture into four patties. Arrange the patties in the crisper tray.

3.Place the crisper tray in the corresponding position in the air fryer. Select Air Fry and cook the burgers for about 15 minutes or until cooked through; make sure to turn them over halfway through the cooking time.

4.Bon appétit!

Nutritional Value (Amount per Serving):

Calories: 517; Fat: 28.81g; Carb: 26.52g; Protein: 35.43g

Pork with Applesauce

Prep Time: 5 Minutes
Cook Time: 55 Minutes
Serves: 5

Ingredients:

- 1 tablespoon olive oil
- 2 tablespoons soy sauce
- 2 pounds (907 g) pork butt
- Kosher salt and freshly ground black pepper, to taste
- 2 cloves garlic, smashed
- 2 sprigs fresh sage, chopped
- 1 cup applesauce

Directions:

1.Start by preheating the air fryer to 360°F (182°C).

2.Toss all ingredients , except for the applesauce, in a lightly greased crisper tray.

3.Place the crisper tray in the corresponding position in the air fryer. Select Air Fry and cook the pork butt for 45 minutes, turning it over halfway through the cooking time.

4.Top the pork butt with the applesauce and continue cooking for a further 10 minutes.

5.Let it rest for a few minutes before slicing and serving. Bon appétit!

Nutritional Value (Amount per Serving):

Calories: 549; Fat: 36g; Carb: 7.48g; Protein: 46.1g

Chapter 2: Beef

Beef Roast with Thyme

Prep Time: 5 Minutes
Cook Time: 55 Minutes
Serves: 4

Ingredients:

- 1½ pounds (680 g) beef eye round roast
- 1 tablespoon olive oil
- Sea salt and ground black pepper, to taste
- 1 onion, sliced
- 1 rosemary sprig
- 1 thyme sprig

Directions:

1.Start by preheating the air fryer to 390°F (199°C).

2.Toss the beef with the olive oil, salt, and black pepper; place the beef in the crisper tray.

3.Place the crisper tray in the corresponding position in the air fryer. Select Roast and cook the beef for 45 minutes, turning it over halfway through the cooking time.chapter

4.Top the beef with the onion, rosemary, and thyme. Continue to cook an additional 10 minutes.

5.Enjoy!

Nutritional Value (Amount per Serving):

Calories: 319; Fat: 10.99g; Carb: 1.27g; Protein: 50.7g

Garlicky Porterhouse Steak

Prep Time: 5 Minutes
Cook Time: 12 Minutes
Serves: 4

Ingredients:

- 1½ pounds (680 g) Porterhouse steak
- 1 tablespoon olive oil
- Kosher salt and ground black pepper, to taste
- ½ teaspoon cayenne pepper
- 1 teaspoon dried parsley
- 1 teaspoon dried oregano
- ½ teaspoon dried basil
- 2 tablespoons butter
- 2 garlic cloves, minced

Directions:

1. Start by preheating the air fryer to 400°F (205°C).

2. Toss the steak with the remaining ingredients; place the steak in the crisper tray.

3. Place the crisper tray in the corresponding position in the air fryer. Select Air Fry and cook the steak for 12 minutes, turning it over halfway through the cooking time.

4. Bon appétit!

Nutritional Value (Amount per Serving):

Calories: 460; Fat: 34.02g; Carb: 1.93g; Protein: 35.1g

Glazed London Broil

Prep Time: 5 Minutes
Cook Time: 28 Minutes
Serves: 3

Ingredients:

- 1 pound (454 g) London broil
- ¼ cup soy sauce
- ¼ cup fresh lemon juice
- 2 garlic cloves, minced
- 1 tablespoon paprika
- Sea salt and ground black pepper, to taste

Directions:

1. Toss the beef with the remaining ingredients and let it marinate for an hour.

2. Preheat the air fryer to 400°F (205°C).

3. Place the beef in a lightly oiled crisper tray and discard the marinade.

4. Place the crisper tray in the corresponding position in the air fryer. Select Roast and cook the beef for 28 minutes, turning it over halfway through the cooking time.

5. Bon appétit!

Nutritional Value (Amount per Serving):

Calories: 390; Fat: 17.83g; Carb: 9.99g; Protein: 48.71g<h2></h2>

Strip Steak with Butter

Prep Time: 5 Minutes
Cook Time: 15 Minutes
Serves: 4

Ingredients:

- 1½ pounds (680 g) New York strip steak

- 2 tablespoons butter, melted

- Sea salt and ground black pepper, to taste

- 1 teaspoon paprika

- 1 teaspoon dried thyme

- 1 teaspoon dried rosemary

Directions:

1.Start by preheating the air fryer to 400°F (205°C).

2.Toss the beef with the remaining ingredients; place the beef in the crisper tray.

3.Place the crisper tray in the corresponding position in the air fryer. Select Air Fry and cook the beef for 15 minutes, turning it over halfway through the cooking time.

4.Enjoy!

Nutritional Value (Amount per Serving):

Calories: 256; Fat: 10.44g; Carb: 1.46g; Protein: 39.63g

Filet Mignon with Herb

Prep Time: 5 Minutes
Cook Time: 14 Minutes
Serves: 4

Ingredients:

- 1½ pounds (680 g) filet mignon
- 2 tablespoons olive oil
- 2 cloves garlic, pressed
- 1 tablespoon Italian herb mix
- 1 teaspoon cayenne pepper
- Kosher salt and freshly ground black pepper, to taste

Directions:

1. Start by preheating the air fryer to 400°F (205°C).

2. Toss the beef with the remaining ingredients; place the beef in the crisper tray.

3. Place the crisper tray in the corresponding position in the air fryer. Select Air Fry and cook the beef for 14 minutes, turning it over halfway through the cooking time.

4. Enjoy!

Nutritional Value (Amount per Serving):

Calories: 290; Fat: 14.76g; Carb: 0.82g; Protein: 38.69g

Ribeye Steak with Rosemary

Prep Time: 5 Minutes
Cook Time: 15 Minutes
Serves: 4

Ingredients:

- 1 pound (454 g) ribeye steak, bone-in

- 2 tablespoons butter, room temperature

- 2 garlic cloves, minced

- Sea salt and ground black pepper, to taste

- 2 rosemary sprigs, leaves picked and chopped

Directions:

1.Start by preheating the air fryer to 400°F (205°C).

2.Toss theribeye steak with the butter, garlic, salt, black pepper, and rosemary; place the steak in the crisper tray.

3.Place the crisper tray in the corresponding position in the air fryer. Select Air Fry and cook the ribeye steak for 15 minutes, turning it over halfway through the cooking time.

4.Bon appétit!

Nutritional Value (Amount per Serving):

Calories: 270; Fat: 18.72g; Carb: 3.55g; Protein: 22.45g

Steak Buns with Mustard

Prep Time: 5 Minutes
Cook Time: 15 Minutes
Serves: 4

Ingredients:

- 1½ pounds (680 g) skirt steak
- 1 teaspoon steak dry rub
- ½ teaspoon cayenne pepper
- Sea salt and ground black pepper, to taste
- 2 tablespoons olive oil
- 2 tablespoons Dijon mustard
- 8 Hawaiian buns

Directions:

1.Start by preheating the air fryer to 400°F (205°C).

2.Toss the beef with the spices and olive oil; place the beef in the crisper tray.

3.Place the crisper tray in the corresponding position in the air fryer. Select Air Fry and cook the beef for 15 minutes, turning it over halfway through the cooking time.

4.Cut the beef into slices and serve them with mustard and Hawaiian buns. Bon appétit!

Nutritional Value (Amount per Serving):

Calories: 480; Fat: 27.94g; Carb: 8.44g; Protein: 46.37g

Beef Roast Rolls

Prep Time: 5 Minutes
Cook Time: 50 Minutes
Serves: 4

Ingredients:

- 1½ pounds (680 g) bottom round roast

- 2 tablespoons olive oil

- 2 garlic cloves, minced

- 1 teaspoon rosemary

- 1 teaspoon parsley

- 1 teaspoon oregano

- Sea salt and freshly ground black pepper, to taste

Directions:

1. Start by preheating the air fryer to 390°F (199°C).

2. Toss the beef with the spices, garlic, and olive oil; place the beef in the crisper tray.

3. Place the crisper tray in the corresponding position in the air fryer. Select Roast and cook the beef for 50 minutes, turning it over halfway through the cooking time.

4. Cut the beef into slices and serve them with dinner rolls. Bon appétit!

Nutritional Value (Amount per Serving):

Calories: 350; Fat: 15.85g; Carb: 0.72g; Protein: 48.25g

Beef Brisket with Thyme

Prep Time: 5 Minutes
Cook Time: 1 Hour
Serves: 4

Ingredients:

- 1½ pounds (680 g) beef brisket
- 2 tablespoons olive oil
- 1 teaspoon onion powder
- 1 teaspoon garlic powder
- Sea salt and ground black pepper, to taste
- 1 teaspoon dried parsley flakes
- 1 teaspoon dried thyme

Directions:

1.Start by preheating the air fryer to 390°F (199°C).

2.Toss the beef with the remaining ingredients; place the beef in the crisper tray.

3.Place the crisper tray in the corresponding position in the air fryer. Select Roast and cook the beef for 15 minutes, turn the beef over and reduce the temperature to 360°F (182°C).

4.Continue to cook the beef for 55 minutes more. Bon appétit!

Nutritional Value (Amount per Serving):

Calories: 406; Fat: 32.14g; Carb: 2.41g; Protein: 25.41g

Garlicky Beef with Mustard

Prep Time: 5 Minutes
Cook Time: 1 Hour
Serves: 4

Ingredients:

- 1½ pounds (680 g) beef brisket
- 2 tablespoons olive oil
- 3 garlic cloves, pressed
- Sea salt and ground black pepper, to taste
- 1 teaspoon crushed red pepper flakes
- 2 tablespoons tomato ketchup
- 2 tablespoons Dijon mustard

Directions:

1.Start by preheating the air fryer to 390°F (199°C).

2.Toss the beef brisket with the olive oil, garlic, salt, black pepper, and red pepper; now, place the beef brisket in the crisper tray.

3.Place the crisper tray in the corresponding position in the air fryer. Select Roast and cook the beef brisket for 15 minutes, turn the beef over and reduce the temperature to 360°F (182°C).

4.Continue to cook the beef brisket for approximately 55 minutes or until cooked through.

5.Shred the beef with two forks; add in the ketchup and mustard and stir to combine well. Bon appétit!

Nutritional Value (Amount per Serving):

ein: 25.88gCalories: 414; Fat: 32.44g; Carb: 3.49g; Prot

Rosemary Beef Roast

Prep Time: 10 Minutes
Cook Time: 55 Minutes
Serves: 5

Ingredients:

- 2 pounds (907 g) top round roast
- 2 tablespoons extra-virgin olive oil
- 2 cloves garlic, pressed
- 1 tablespoon chopped fresh rosemary
- 1 tablespoon chopped fresh parsley
- 1 teaspoon red chili powder
- Kosher salt and freshly ground black pepper, to taste

Directions:

1. Start by preheating the air fryer to 390°F (199°C).

2. Toss the beef with the remaining ingredients; place the beef in the crisper tray.

3. Place the crisper tray in the corresponding position in the air fryer. Select Roast and cook the beef for 55 minutes, turning it over halfway through the cooking time.

4. Enjoy!

Nutritional Value (Amount per Serving):

Calories: 236; Fat: 6.95g; Carb: 0.78g; Protein: 43.01g

Beef Burgers Buns

Prep Time: 5 Minutes
Cook Time: 15 Minutes
Serves: 3

Ingredients:

- ¾ pound (340 g) ground beef
- 2 tablespoons minced onion
- 1 teaspoon minced garlic
- 1 teaspoon cayenne pepper
- Sea salt and ground black pepper, to taste
- 1 teaspoon red chili powder
- 3 hamburger buns

Directions:

1.Start by preheating the air fryer to 380°F (193°C).

2.Mix the beef, onion, garlic, cayenne pepper, salt, black pepper, and red chili powder until everything is well combined. Form the mixture into three patties. Place the patties in the crisper tray.

3.Place the crisper tray in the corresponding position in the air fryer. Select Air Fry and cook the burgers for about 15 minutes or until cooked through; make sure to turn them over halfway through the cooking time.

4.Serve the burgers on the prepared buns and enjoy!

Nutritional Value (Amount per Serving):

Calories: 442; Fat: 20.49g; Carb: 28.21g; Protein: 34.19g

Lemony London Broil

Prep Time: 10 Minutes
Cook Time: 28 Minutes
Serves: 4

Ingredients:

- 1 pound (454 g) London broil
- Kosher salt and ground black pepper, to taste
- 2 tablespoons olive oil
- 1 small lemon, freshly squeezed
- 3 cloves garlic, minced
- 1 tablespoon chopped fresh parsley
- 1 tablespoon chopped fresh coriander

Directions:

1. Toss the beef with the remaining ingredients and let it marinate for an hour.

2. Preheat the air fryer to 400°F (205°C).

3. Place the beef in a lightly oiled crisper tray and discard the marinade.

4. Place the crisper tray in the corresponding position in the air fryer. Select Roast and cook the beef for 28 minutes, turning it over halfway through the cooking time.

5. Bon appétit!

Nutritional Value (Amount per Serving):

Calories: 302; Fat: 17.03g; Carb: 2.71g; Protein: 35.22g

Shallots Beef Meatloaf

Prep Time: 10 Minutes
Cook Time: 25 Minutes
Serves: 4

Ingredients:

- 1½ pounds (680 g) ground chuck

- 1 egg, beaten

- 2 tablespoons olive oil

- 4 tablespoons crushed crackers

- ½ cup minced shallots

- 2 garlic cloves, minced

- 1 tablespoon chopped fresh rosemary

- 1 tablespoon chopped fresh thyme

- Sea salt and ground black pepper, to taste

Directions:

1.Start by preheating the air fryer to 390°F (199°C).

2.Thoroughly combine all ingredients until everything is well combined.

3.Scrape the beef mixture into a lightly oiled baking pan.

4.Place the baking pan in the corresponding position in the air fryer. Select Bake and cook the meatloaf for 25 minutes. Bon appétit!

Nutritional Value (Amount per Serving):

Calories: 374; Fat: 23.11g; Carb: 5.46g; Protein: 36.49g

Skirt Steak with Garlic

Prep Time: 5 Minutes
Cook Time: 12 Minutes
Serves: 4

Ingredients:

- 1½ pounds (680 g) skirt steak
- Kosher salt and freshly cracked black pepper, to taste
- 1 teaspoon cayenne pepper
- ¼ teaspoon cumin powder
- 2 tablespoons olive oil
- 2 garlic cloves, minced

Directions:

1.Start by preheating the air fryer to 400°F (205°C).

2.Toss the steak with the other ingredients; place the steak in the crisper tray.

3.Place the crisper tray in the corresponding position in the air fryer. Select Air Fry and cook the steak for 12 minutes, turning it over halfway through the cooking time.

4.Bon appétit!

Nutritional Value (Amount per Serving):

Calories: 443; Fat: 27.38g; Carb: 1.87g; Protein: 44.84g

Beef Filet Mignon with Mustard

Prep Time: 5 Minutes
Cook Time: 14 Minutes
Serves: 4

Ingredients:

- 1 pound (454 g) beef filet mignon
- Sea salt and ground black pepper, to taste
- 1 teaspoon cayenne pepper
- 3 tablespoons olive oil
- 1 tablespoon Dijon mustard
- 4 tablespoons dry French wine

Directions:

1.Start by preheating the air fryer to 400°F (205°C).

2.Toss the filet mignon with the rest of the ingredients; place the filet mignon in the crisper tray.

3.Place the crisper tray in the corresponding position in the air fryer. Select Air Fry and cook the filet mignon for 14 minutes, turning it over halfway through the cooking time.

4.Enjoy!

Nutritional Value (Amount per Serving):

Calories: 249; Fat: 15.64g; Carb: 1.75g; Protein: 26.19g

Ribeye Steak with Butter

Prep Time: 5 Minutes
Cook Time: 15 Minutes
Serves: 4

Ingredients:

- 1½ pounds (680 g) ribeye steak, bone-in

- 2 tablespoons butter

- 1 Montreal seasoning mix

- Sea salt and ground black pepper, to taste

Directions:

1.Start by preheating the air fryer to 400°F (205°C).

2.Toss theribeye steak with the remaining ingredients; place the ribeye steak in a lightly oiled crisper tray.

3.Place the crisper tray in the corresponding position in the air fryer. Select Air Fry and cook the ribeye steak for 15 minutes, turning it over halfway through the cooking time.

4.Bon appétit!

Nutritional Value (Amount per Serving):

Calories: 373; Fat: 25.17g; Carb: 4.05g; Protein: 33.39g

Red Wine Rump Roast

Prep Time: 5 Minutes
Cook Time: 55 Minutes
Serves: 4

Ingredients:

- 1½ pounds (680 g) rump roast

- 2 tablespoons olive oil

- Sea salt and ground black pepper, to taste

- 1 teaspoon Italian seasoning mix

- 1 onion, sliced

- 2 cloves garlic, peeled

- ¼ cup red wine

Directions:

1.Start by preheating the air fryer to 390°F (199°C).

2.Toss therump roast with the rest of the ingredients; place the rump roast in a lightly oiled crisper tray.

3.Place the crisper tray in the corresponding position in the air fryer. Select Roast and cook the rump roast for 55 minutes, turning it over halfway through the cooking time.

4.Bon appétit!

Nutritional Value (Amount per Serving):

Calories: 268; Fat: 13.06g; Carb: 3.32g; Protein: 32.06g

Tenderloin Steaks with Mushrooms

Prep Time: 10 Minutes
Cook Time: 15 Minutes
Serves: 4

Ingredients:

- 1½ pounds (680 g) tenderloin steaks

- 2 tablespoons butter, melted

- 1 teaspoon garlic powder

- ½ teaspoon mustard powder

- 1 teaspoon cayenne pepper

- Sea salt and ground black pepper, to taste

- ½ pound (227 g) cremini mushrooms, sliced

Directions:

1.Start by preheating the air fryer to 400°F (205°C).

2.Toss the beef with 1 tablespoon of the butter and spices; place the beef in the crisper tray.

3.Place the crisper tray in the corresponding position in the air fryer. Select Roast and cook the beef for 10 minutes, turning it over halfway through the cooking time.

4.Add in the mushrooms along with the remaining 1 tablespoon of the butter. Continue to cook an additional 5 minutes. Serve warm.

5.Bon appétit!

Nutritional Value (Amount per Serving):

Calories: 651; Fat: 37.85g; Carb: 44.66g; Protein: 38.87g

Beef Brisket with BBQ Sauce

Prep Time: 5 Minutes
Cook Time: 1 Hour
Serves: 4

Ingredients:

- 1½ pounds (680 g) beef brisket

- ¼ cup barbecue sauce

- 2 tablespoons soy sauce

Directions:

1.Start by preheating the air fryer to 390°F (199°C).

2.Toss the beef with the remaining ingredients; place the beef in the crisper tray.

3.Place the crisper tray in the corresponding position in the air fryer. Select Roast and cook the beef for 15 minutes, turn the beef over and reduce the temperature to 360°F (182°C).

4.Continue to cook the beef for 55 minutes more. Bon appétit!

Nutritional Value (Amount per Serving):

Calories: 391; Fat: 26.9g; Carb: 9.51g; Protein: 25.69g

Beef Roast with Carrot

Prep Time: 10 Minutes
Cook Time: 55 Minutes
Serves: 5

Ingredients:

- 2 pounds (907 g) top sirloin roast
- 2 tablespoons olive oil
- Sea salt and ground black pepper, to taste
- 2 carrots, sliced
- 1 tablespoon fresh coriander
- 1 tablespoon fresh thyme
- 1 tablespoon fresh rosemary

Directions:

1. Start by preheating the air fryer to 390°F (199°C).

2. Toss the beef with the olive oil, salt, and black pepper; place the beef in the crisper tray.

3. Place the crisper tray in the corresponding position in the air fryer. Select Roast and cook the beef for 45 minutes, turning it over halfway through the cooking time.

4. Top the beef with the carrots and herbs. Continue to cook an additional 10 minutes.

5. Enjoy!

Nutritional Value (Amount per Serving):

Calories: 466; Fat: 28.86g; Carb: 2.98g; Protein: 49.22g

Beef Cheeseburgers Buns

Prep Time: 5 Minutes
Cook Time: 15 Minutes
Serves: 3

Ingredients:

- ¾ pound (340 g) ground chuck

- 1 teaspoon minced garlic

- 2 tablespoons BBQ sauce

- Sea salt and ground black pepper, to taste

- 3 slices cheese

- 3 hamburger buns

Directions:

1.Start by preheating the air fryer to 380°F (193°C).

2.Mix the ground chuck, garlic, BBQ sauce, salt, and black pepper until everything is well combined. Form the mixture into four patties.

3.Arrange the patties in the crisper tray.

4.Place the crisper tray in the corresponding position in the air fryer. Select Air Fry and cook the burgers for about 15 minutes or until cooked through; make sure to turn them over halfway through the cooking time.

5.Top each burger with cheese. Serve the burgers on the prepared buns and enjoy!

Nutritional Value (Amount per Serving):

Calories: 463; Fat: 18.47g; Carb: 38.94g; Protein: 35g

Butter London Broil

Prep Time: 5 Minutes
Cook Time: 28 Minutes
Serves: 4

Ingredients:

- 1½ pounds (680 g) London broil
- Kosher salt and ground black pepper, to taste
- ¼ teaspoon ground bay leaf
- 3 tablespoons butter
- 1 tablespoon Dijon mustard
- 1 teaspoon crushed garlic
- 1 tablespoon chopped fresh parsley

Directions:

1.Start by preheating the air fryer to 400°F (205°C).

2.Toss the beef with the salt and black pepper; place the beef in a lightly oiled crisper tray.

3.Place the crisper tray in the corresponding position in the air fryer. Select Roast and cook the beef for 28 minutes, turning over halfway through the cooking time.

4.In the meantime, mix the butter with the remaining ingredients and place it in the refrigerator until well chilled.

5.Serve warm beef with the chilled garlic butter on the side. Bon appétit!

Nutritional Value (Amount per Serving):

Calories: 432; Fat: 24.12g; Carb: 1.63g; Protein: 52.71g

Beef Brisket Carnitas

Prep Time: 5 Minutes
Cook Time: 1 Hour
Serves: 4

Ingredients:

- 1½ pounds (680 g) beef brisket
- 2 tablespoons olive oil
- Sea salt and ground black pepper, to taste
- 1 teaspoon chili powder
- 4 medium-sized flour tortillas

Directions:

1.Start by preheating the air fryer to 390°F (199°C).

2.Toss the beef brisket with the olive oil, salt, black pepper, and chili powder; now, place the beef brisket in the crisper tray.

3.Place the crisper tray in the corresponding position in the air fryer. Select Roast and cook the beef brisket for 15 minutes, turn the beef over and reduce the temperature to 360°F (182°C).

4.Continue to cook the beef brisket for approximately 55 minutes or until cooked through.

5.Shred the beef with two forks and serve with tortillas and toppings of choice. Bon appétit!

Nutritional Value (Amount per Serving):

Calories: 541; Fat: 34.97g; Carb: 25.69g; Protein: 29.01g

Flank Steak with Paprika

Prep Time: 5 Minutes
Cook Time: 12 Minutes
Serves: 5

Ingredients:

- 2 pounds (907 g) flank steak

- 2 tablespoons olive oil

- 1 teaspoon paprika

- Sea salt and ground black pepper, to taste

Directions:

1.Start by preheating the air fryer to 400°F (205°C).

2.Toss the steak with the remaining ingredients; place the steak in the crisper tray.

3.Place the crisper tray in the corresponding position in the air fryer. Select Air Fry and cook the steak for 12 minutes, turning over halfway through the cooking time.

4.Bon appétit!

Nutritional Value (Amount per Serving):

Calories: 301; Fat: 14.55g; Carb: 1.1g; Protein: 39.13g

Spicy Beef Meatloaf

Prep Time: 10 Minutes
Cook Time: 25 Minutes
Serves: 4

Ingredients:

- 1½ pounds (680 g) ground chuck
- ½ onion, chopped
- 1 teaspoon minced habanero pepper
- ¼ cup crushed tortilla chips
- 1 teaspoon minced garlic
- Sea salt and ground black pepper, to taste
- 2 tablespoons olive oil
- 1 egg, whisked

Directions:

1.Start by preheating the air fryer to 390°F (199°C).

2.Thoroughly combine all ingredients until everything is well combined.

3.Scrape the beef mixture into a lightly oiled baking pan.

4.Place the baking pan in the corresponding position in the air fryer. Select Bake and cook the meatloaf for 25 minutes. Bon appétit!

Nutritional Value (Amount per Serving):

Calories: 372; Fat: 22.81g; Carb: 5.58g; Protein: 36.49g

Filet Mignon with Basil

Prep Time: 5 Minutes
Cook Time: 14 Minutes
Serves: 4

Ingredients:

- 1½ pounds (680 g) filet mignon Georgia

- Sea salt and ground black pepper, to taste Georgia

- 2 tablespoons olive oil Georgia

- 1 teaspoon dried rosemary Georgia

- 1 teaspoon dried thyme Georgia

- 1 teaspoon dried basil Georgia

- 2 cloves garlic, minced Georgia

Directions:

1.Start by preheating the air fryer to 400°F (205°C).Georgia

2.Toss the beef with the remaining ingredients; place the beef in the crisper tray.Georgia

3.Place the crisper tray in the corresponding position in the air fryer. Select Air Fry and cook the beef for 14 minutes, turning it over halfway through the cooking time.Georgia

4.Enjoy!Georgia

Nutritional Value (Amount per Serving):

Calories:293; Fat: 14.73g; Carb: 1.8g; Protein: 38.92g

Beef Cheese Muffins

Prep Time: 10 Minutes
Cook Time: 25 Minutes
Serves: 4

Ingredients:

- Meatloaves:

- 1 pound (454 g) ground beef

- ¼ cup seasoned bread crumbs

- ¼ cup grated Parmesan cheese

- 1 small onion, minced

- 2 garlic cloves, pressed

- 1 egg, beaten

- Sea salt and ground black pepper, to taste

- Glaze:

- 4 tablespoons tomato sauce

- 1 tablespoon brown sugar

- 1 tablespoon Dijon mustard

Directions:

1.Start by preheating the air fryer to 380°F (193°C).

2.Thoroughly combine all ingredients for the meatloaves until everything is well combined.

3.Scrape the beef mixture into lightly oiled silicone cups and transfer them to the baking pan.

4.Place the baking pan in the corresponding position in the air fryer. Select Bake and cook the beef cups for 20 minutes.

5.In the meantime, mix the remaining ingredients for the glaze. Then, spread the glaze on top of each muffin; continue to cook for another 5 minutes.

6.Bon appétit!

Nutritional Value (Amount per Serving):

Calories: 349; Fat: 17.04g; Carb: 11g; Protein: 35.48g

Ribeye Steak with Cheese

Prep Time: 5 Minutes
Cook Time: 15 Minutes
Serves: 4

Ingredients:

- 1 pound (454 g) ribeye steak, bone-in
- Sea salt and ground black pepper, to taste
- 2 tablespoons olive oil
- ½ teaspoon onion powder
- 1 teaspoon garlic powder
- 1 cup crumbled blue cheese

Directions:

1.Start by preheating the air fryer to 400°F (205°C).

2.Toss theribeye steak with the salt, black pepper, olive oil, onion powder, and garlic powder; place the ribeye steak in the crisper tray.

3.Place the crisper tray in the corresponding position in the air fryer. Select Air Fry and cook the ribeye steak for 15 minutes, turning it over halfway through the cooking time.

4.Top the ribeye steak with the cheese and serve warm. Bon appétit!

Nutritional Value (Amount per Serving):

Calories: 399; Fat: 29.41g; Carb: 4.64g; Protein: 29.67g

Rump Roast with Paprika

Prep Time: 5 Minutes
Cook Time: 50 Minutes
Serves: 4

Ingredients:

- 1½ pounds (680 g) rump roast

- Ground black pepper and kosher salt, to taste

- 1 teaspoon paprika

- 2 tablespoons olive oil

- ¼ cup brandy

- 2 tablespoons cold butter

Directions:

1.Start by preheating the air fryer to 390°F (199°C).

2.Toss therump roast with the black pepper, salt, paprika, olive oil, and brandy; place the rump roast in a lightly oiled crisper tray.

3.Place the crisper tray in the corresponding position in the air fryer. Select Roast and cook for 50 minutes, turning it over halfway through the cooking time.

4.Serve with the cold butter and enjoy!

Nutritional Value (Amount per Serving):

Calories: 329; Fat: 18.9g; Carb: 3.18g; Protein: 32.06g

Coulotte Roast with Garlic

Prep Time: 10 Minutes
Cook Time: 55 Minutes
Serves: 5

Ingredients:

- 2 pounds (907 g) Coulotte roast
- 2 tablespoons olive oil
- 1 tablespoon finely chopped fresh parsley
- 1 tablespoon finely chopped fresh cilantro
- 2 garlic cloves, minced
- Kosher salt and ground black pepper, to taste

Directions:

1.Start by preheating the air fryer to 390°F (199°C).

2.Toss the roast beef with the remaining ingredients; place the roast beef in the crisper tray.

3.Place the crisper tray in the corresponding position in the air fryer. Select Roast and cook for 55 minutes, turning over halfway through the cooking time.

4.Enjoy!

Nutritional Value (Amount per Serving):

Calories: 262; Fat: 12.13g; Carb: 2.46g; Protein: 34.07g

Garlicky Beef Tenderloin

Prep Time: 10 Minutes
Cook Time: 20 Minutes
Serves: 4

Ingredients:

- 1½ pounds (680 g) beef tenderloin, sliced

- 2 tablespoons sesame oil

- 1 teaspoon five-spice powder

- 2 garlic cloves, minced

- 1 teaspoon peeled and grated fresh ginger

- 2 tablespoons soy sauce

Directions:

1.Start by preheating the air fryer to 400°F (205°C).

2.Toss the beef tenderloin with the remaining ingredients; place the beef tenderloin in the crisper tray.

3.Place the crisper tray in the corresponding position in the air fryer. Select Air Fry and cook the beef tenderloin for 20 minutes, turning it over halfway through the cooking time.

4.Enjoy!

Nutritional Value (Amount per Serving):

Calories: 447; Fat: 23.42g; Carb: 3.04g; Protein: 52.62g

Beef Steaks with Fish Sauce

Prep Time: 5 Minutes
Cook Time: 14 Minutes
Serves: 4

Ingredients:

- 1½ pounds (680 g) Tomahawk steaks

- 2 bell peppers, sliced

- 2 tablespoons butter, melted

- 2 teaspoons Montreal steak seasoning

- 2 tablespoons fish sauce

- Sea salt and ground black pepper, to taste

Directions:

1.Start by preheating the air fryer to 400°F (205°C).

2.Toss all ingredients in the crisper tray.

3.Place the crisper tray in the corresponding position in the air fryer. Select Air Fry and cook the steak and peppers for about 14 minutes, turning it over halfway through the cooking time.

4.Bon appétit!

Nutritional Value (Amount per Serving):

Calories: 526; Fat: 35.92g; Carb: 4.35g; Protein: 43.9g

Mushroom and Beef Patties Rolls

Prep Time: 5 Minutes
Cook Time: 15 Minutes
Serves: 4

Ingredients:

- 1 pound (454 g) ground chuck

- 2 garlic cloves, minced

- 1 small onion, chopped

- 1 cup chopped mushrooms

- 1 teaspoon cayenne pepper

- Sea salt and ground black pepper, to taste

- 4 brioche rolls

Directions:

1.Start by preheating the air fryer to 380°F (193°C).

2.Mix the ground chuck, garlic, onion, mushrooms, cayenne pepper, salt, and black pepper until everything is well combined. Form the mixture into four patties.

3.Arrange the patties in the crisper tray.

4.Place the crisper tray in the corresponding position in the air fryer. Select Air Fry and cook the patties for about 15 minutes or until cooked through; make sure to turn them over halfway through the cooking time.

5.Serve the patties on the prepared brioche rolls and enjoy!

Nutritional Value (Amount per Serving):

Calories: 305; Fat: 10.47g; Carb: 25.29g; Protein: 27.75g

Steak Salad with Tomato

Prep Time: 10 Minutes
Cook Time: 12 Minutes
Serves: 5

Ingredients:

- 2 pounds (907 g) T-bone steak

- 1 teaspoon garlic powder

- Sea salt and ground black pepper, to taste

- 2 tablespoons lime juice

- ¼ cup extra-virgin olive oil

- 1 bell pepper, seeded and sliced

- 1 red onion, sliced

- 1 tomato, diced

Directions:

1.Start by preheating the air fryer to 400°F (205°C).

2.Toss the steak with the garlic powder, salt, and black pepper; place the steak in the crisper tray.

3.Place the crisper tray in the corresponding position in the air fryer. Select Air Fry and cook the steak for 12 minutes, turning it over halfway through the cooking time.

4.Cut the steak into slices and add in the remaining ingredients. Serve at room temperature or well chilled.

5.Bon appétit!

Nutritional Value (Amount per Serving):

Calories: 424; Fat: 23.13g; Carb: 3.79g; Protein: 51.26g

Conclusion

Oster Digital French Door Oven is one of the versatile kitchen appliances that perform numerous functions successfully. Follow this cookbook with straightforward instructions, encouraging advice, and time saving tips make meal planning, preparation, and cooking that much easier.

The cookbook will take your kitchen skills to a whole new level. This tasty collection of healthy recipes will make you proficient in oven cooking. Pick up your copy today and let you start cooking amazing Oster Digital French Door Oven recipes.

CPSIA information can be obtained
at www.ICGtesting.com
Printed in the USA
BVHW022307050723
666779BV00013B/366